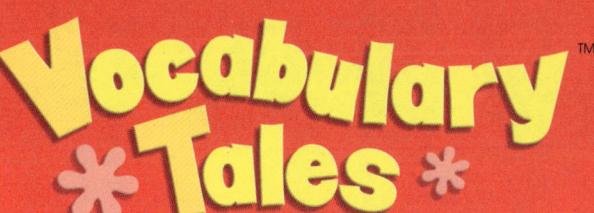

MW01613690

Squirrel's Tree

by Pamela Chanko
illustrated by Steve Cox

SCHOLASTIC INC.

New York • Toronto • London • Auckland • Sydney
Mexico City • New Delhi • Hong Kong • Buenos Aires

No part of this publication may be reproduced, stored in a retrieval system, or transmitted in any form or by any means, electronic, mechanical, photocopying, recording, or otherwise, without written permission of the publisher. For information regarding permission, write to Scholastic Inc., Attention: Permissions Department, 557 Broadway, New York, NY 10012.

Designed by Maria Lilja
ISBN-13: 978-0-545-08856-5 • ISBN-10: 0-545-08856-9
Copyright © 2009 by Scholastic Inc.
All rights reserved. Printed in China.

SCHOLASTIC, VOCABULARY TALES™, and associated logos are trademarks and/or registered trademarks of Scholastic Inc.

First printing, January 2009
12 11 10 9 8 7 6 5 4 3 2 1   9 10 11 12 13 14/0

Building Vocabulary With This Book
This book contains eight key words that are important for all children to know. Read the story straight through for enjoyment. Then read it again, pausing to define and discuss each key word. Follow-up the tale with the fun activities on pages 14–16. When you're done, celebrate—kids will have added eight great words to their vocabularies!

This is Squirrel's favorite tree.
He loves it for a reason.

It's the perfect place to be,
in each amazing **season**!

KEY WORD: **season**

Simple Definition: one of the four natural parts of the year; the four *seasons* are winter, spring, summer, and fall

Sample Sentence: I love snow, so winter is my favorite *season*.

In winter, every branch is bare,
and snow is on the ground.

KEY WORD: **shiver**

Simple Definition: to shake with cold or fear

Sample Sentence: Maria started to *shiver* when she took off her warm mittens.

But Squirrel doesn't shake and **shiver**, because he's safe and sound.

KEY WORD: bloom

Simple Definition: to burst with flowers

Sample Sentence: I can't wait for my garden to *bloom* in the spring.

In spring, the tree begins to **bloom**, and birds come flying home.

KEY WORD: scamper

Simple Definition: to run lightly and quickly

Sample Sentence: I watched the child *scamper* off to play.

Bunnies **scamper** here and there—
Squirrel knows he's not alone!

7

KEY WORD: **lazy**

Simple Definition: not wanting to work or be active

Sample Sentence: I was feeling *lazy*, so I did not want to clean my room.

In the **lazy** days of summer,
when the air is very hot,

8

KEY WORD: **shade**

Simple Definition: a cool, dark area away from the sun's bright light

Sample Sentence: You can cool off on a hot day by resting in the *shade*.

the tree gives Squirrel some **shade**, which really helps a lot!

KEY WORD: autumn

Simple Definition: the season between summer and winter, also called *fall*

Sample Sentence: Every *autumn*, I help my dad rake the leaves in our yard.

When **autumn** comes, the colors change, and leaves fall to the ground.

KEY WORD: **gather**

Simple Definition: to collect or pick things

Sample Sentence: On a nature walk, you can *gather* different kinds of leaves.

Lots of nuts drop from the tree.
Squirrel **gathers** them around.

Squirrel stores up all the nuts he finds,
and guess what he does then?

He stays inside his favorite tree,
until spring comes back again!

Meaning Match

Listen to the definition. Then go to the WORD CHEST and find a vocabulary word that matches it.

1. to shake with cold or fear
2. a cool, dark area away from the sun's bright light
3. one of the four natural parts of the year
4. to collect or pick things
5. to run lightly and quickly
6. to burst with flowers
7. not wanting to work or be active
8. the season between summer and winter, also called *fall*

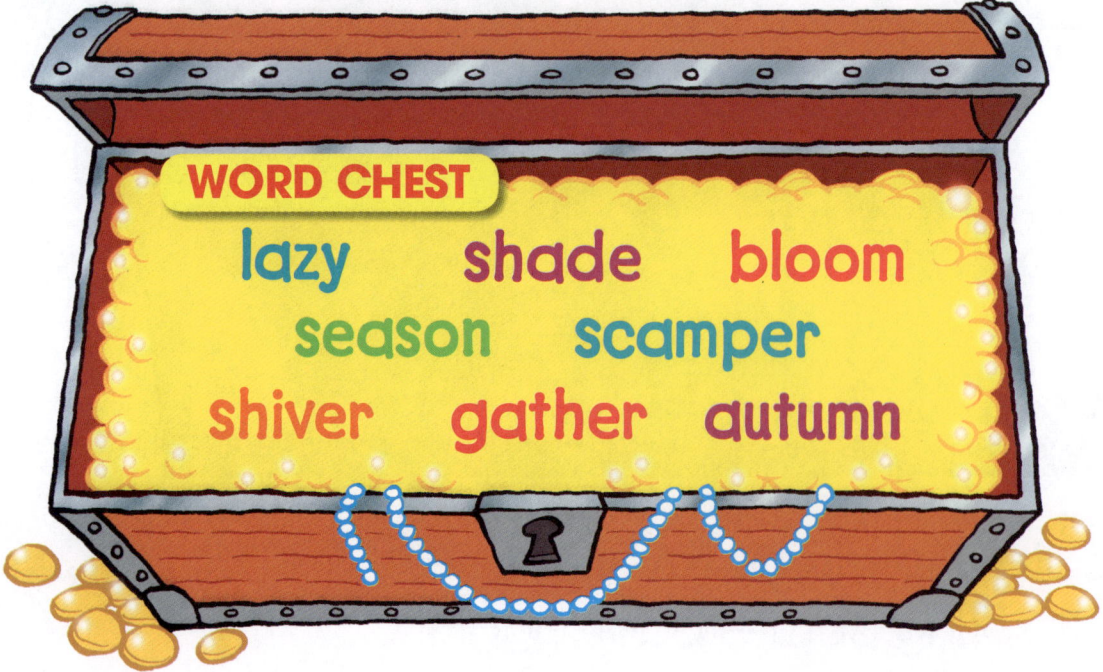

WORD CHEST

lazy   shade   bloom

season   scamper

shiver   gather   autumn

14

Answers: 1. shiver 2. shade 3. season 4. gather 5. scamper 6. bloom 7. lazy 8. autumn

Vocabulary Fill-ins

Listen to the sentence. Then go to the WORD BOX and find the best word to fill in the blank.

WORD BOX

autumn	gather	season	bloom
scamper	shade	shiver	lazy

1. Squirrels love to _____ around the park.

2. If you sit in the _____, you won't get a sunburn.

3. In _____, the leaves change color and fall from the trees.

4. My cat sleeps all day long. She is so _____!

5. Leo likes to walk on the hillside and _____ blueberries.

6. Summer is the best _____ to go to the beach.

7. After swimming, the cold air made Shelly _____.

8. The tree was covered in beautiful flowers. It had begun to _____!

Vocabulary Questions

Listen to each question. Think about it. Then answer.

1 When it is hot out, would you rather be in the sun or in the **shade**? Why?

2 What is your favorite **season**? What do you like about it?

3 When is the last time you were **lazy**? Why did you feel that way?

4 What special activities can you do in the **autumn**? What holidays come at this time of year?

5 Can you name five animals that like to **scamper**?

6 What makes you **shiver**? Make a list.

7 What are some things you might **gather** on a walk through the park?

8 Pretend you are a flower about to **bloom**. Act it out.

Extra: Can you think of some more seasonal words? Make a list.